for Harlem
past, present, future
—R.W.

for Gaga—happy 101st birthday
—C.R.

Text copyright © 2012 by Renée Watson
Jacket art and interior illustrations copyright © 2012 by Christian Robinson

Visit us on the Web!
randomhouse.com/kids

Educators and librarians, for a variety of teaching tools,
visit us at randomhouse.com/teachers

Library of Congress Cataloging-in-Publication Data
Watson, Renee.
Harlem's little blackbird / Renée Watson ; illustrated by Christian Robinson. — 1st ed.
p. cm.
ISBN 978-0-375-86973-0 (trade) — ISBN 978-0-375-96973-7 (lib. bdg.)
1. Mills, Florence, 1896–1927—Juvenile literature.
2. African American singers—New York (State)—New York—Biography—Juvenile literature.
3. Singers—New York (State)—New York—Biography—Juvenile literature.
I. Robinson, Christian, ill. II. Title.
ML3930.M63W37 2012
782.42165092—dc23
[B] 2011043314

MANUFACTURED IN CHINA
10 9 8 7 6 5 4 3 2 1
First Edition

HARLEM'S LITTLE BLACKBIRD

Words by Renée Watson
Pictures by Christian Robinson

RANDOM HOUSE  NEW YORK

They called her Harlem's Little Blackbird. Her name was Florence Mills. She was born in 1896 and lived in a teeny-tiny, itsy-bitsy house in Washington, DC. A house so fragile, it would shake whenever a thunderstorm came.

Mother said, "Don't fear." And she would sway back and forth to the rain's rhythm, singing the same spirituals that had carried her family through slavery's storms.

When peace, like a river, attendeth my way,
When sorrows like sea billows roll;
Whatever my lot, Thou hast taught me to say,
It is well, it is well, with my soul.

Mother's voice wrapped Florence like a warm blanket. Florence started singing too. The louder the thunder roared, the stronger she sang. Soon the storm faded to a damp drizzle, and then the drizzle disappeared. Her voice had chased the storm away.

Florence thought,

If my voice is powerful enough to stop the rain, what else can it do?

It wasn't long before Florence found out.

On the playground at school, she would sing and dance. Her friends would stop playing just to listen. Whenever music would play, Florence's hands got to waving, her hips got to shaking, and her feet strutted and glided across the pavement. The cakewalk is what they called it.

Everyone was cakewalking, but Florence did it best. Her feet were like wings fluttering in the air. Soon Florence was cakewalking and singing in contests all over town. She won many medals.

Florence had a hard time paying attention in school.
Instead of listening to the teacher, she would stare out
the window. The sky became her stage, and she was a
star singing and dancing for the world.

But wishing couldn't change the fact that she was just
Florence Mills, the daughter of former slaves, living in
a teeny-tiny, itsy-bitsy house.

Word danced around Washington about the little girl with big talent. Florence was invited to perform at a fancy theater. The night before the show, she practiced her routine over and over.

On the day of the show, when Florence and her friends arrived at the theater, nothing was what Florence had dreamed it would be.

"*They* can't come in!" the manager said. He pointed to the sign that read WHITES ONLY. "No Negroes in the audience!"

Florence used her voice to stand up for what was right.

"If they can't go *in there,* I'm staying *out here*!" Florence said. And with her hands on her hips and her head held high, she walked away.

"Wait!" the manager yelled. But Florence kept walking. He begged her to perform and snuck her friends in to see the show.

That night, Florence performed her best routine.
Everyone stood and clapped.

Less than six years later, her family moved to New York City. Florence and her sisters became a singing and dancing trio, the Mills Sisters. They performed at Harlem's Lincoln Theatre.

In the summer, the Mills Sisters spent their days at Coney Island. Florence never got tired of going on the rides and playing games at the arcades. But nothing was as fun as performing at the Surf Avenue Opera House.

Reporters followed them everywhere, and there was one sister they adored the most. Sixteen-year-old Florence.

"Come hear the woman who sings like a bird!"

"When she dances, it's as if she's flying!"

And she was!

She flew from stage to stage, all over the country from the East Coast to the West Coast, until she landed at New York's 63rd Street Music Hall. It was 1921, and Florence won a role in *Shuffle Along*. The sold-out show introduced jazz to white audiences.

Each night, Florence gave her best. Every part of her body danced. Her eyelashes fluttered, her fingers wiggled. She whirled around and boogied down. Night after night, she gave the audience a hand-clapping, foot-stomping good time.

A very special thing was happening in Harlem. The Harlem Renaissance. All kinds of creative minds contributed to Harlem's cultural movement. Langston Hughes penned poetry. Duke Ellington composed jazz classics. And in play after play, Florence continued to mesmerize crowds. In *From Dover Street to Dixie*, she was so good, the cast was invited to London. Florence was excited to travel overseas.

But not everyone welcomed her. When she boarded the ship, the white passengers refused to eat in the same dining room as Florence and her troupe.

When she arrived in London, many people threatened to boycott the show because they didn't want to see black performers on their stage. On opening night, Florence took a deep breath, opened her mouth, and sang one note, then another, and another. The audience was amazed.

Each night when Florence stepped onstage, the audience cheered
before she even opened her mouth. She was an international star.
And Florence thought,

If my voice can take me around the world,
what else can it do?

After Florence sailed back to Harlem, Mr. Ziegfeld, an important Broadway manager, offered Florence a leading role. She would have been the first black woman to star in the Ziegfeld Follies. It was every performer's dream, but she turned it down.

Instead she chose to use her voice in shows that gave unknown black singers and actors a chance to perform onstage. Florence became the leading lady in *Dixie to Broadway*. One hundred lights shined on the marquee, flashing her name.

The daughter of former slaves, who grew up in a teeny-tiny, itsy-bitsy house, had made it.

Florence wanted to use her voice for more than entertainment. In the show *Blackbirds* she sang "I'm a Little Blackbird Looking for a Bluebird." It became her favorite song to perform—a cry for equal rights.

Tho' I'm of a darker hue,
I've a heart the same as you....
For love I'm dyin', my heart is cryin'.
A wise old owl said Keep on tryin'.
I'm a little blackbird looking for a bluebird too....

The show was such a hit that Florence was invited to London again. This time, she was welcomed by photographers and news reporters, and she was invited to many parties.

After her performances, Florence disguised herself so no one would recognize her. She went to hospitals to deliver flowers to patients. And she walked along the Thames River giving money and food to beggars.

Florence kept giving, and dancing, and singing until she was too exhausted to perform anymore. She became very ill and returned to Harlem to receive treatment from her doctor. But there was not much her doctor could do.

On November 1, 1927, Florence's song came to an end.

More than 150,000 mourners flooded the streets of Harlem to say goodbye. Letters, telegrams, and flowers were sent to the family from all over the world. People who had a lot and people who had little, politicians and entertainers,

Even blackbirds came. Hundreds of them were seen hovering nearby.

Florence's dream lives on in the singers and dancers who came after her. It lives on in the heart of every boy and girl from a teeny-tiny, itsy-bitsy place who dreams of doing great big, gigantic, enormous things.

AUTHOR'S NOTE

Florence's voice was never recorded, and no films of her performances exist. So how do we know how great she was?

The answers lie in the reaction her peers had to her. Florence was so great, Duke Ellington composed the song "Black Beauty" as a tribute to her. Iconic performers Lena Horne and Paul Robeson said she was one of the best. In 1925, Florence became the first black woman to be photographed for a full spread in *Vanity Fair*. When *Blackbirds* moved to London's Pavilion Theatre, the Prince of Wales saw the show more than twenty times.

But her talent wasn't all that made Florence great. What made her a remarkable woman was that she used her fame and fortune to help others. If you were a young child playing on the streets of Harlem or sitting on the stoop of a brownstone, Florence might stop by and give you candy. If you were a guest at an NAACP fund-raising event, you might hear Florence as one of the featured performers. These are the things that made Florence a beloved entertainer. Her talent, yes, but mostly her generosity and her faith.

I would like to thank Suzy Capozzi, my editor at Random House, for introducing me to Florence; Bill Egan, author of *Florence Mills: Harlem Jazz Queen,* for sharing his invaluable knowledge with me; and the Schomburg Center for Research in Black Culture for keeping Florence's legacy alive in its research collection.